Inspiring
Women
Every Day

March

REVELATION

....

AMY BOUCHER PYE

April

REFLECTIVE ROUTINE AND
RADICAL REST

....

NAOMI AIDOO

MIX
Paper from
responsible sources
FSC® C021017
www.fsc.org

WAVERLEY ABBEY
RESOURCES

Amy Boucher Pye

Amy Boucher Pye is a writer, speaker and spiritual director and the author of *7 Ways to Pray* (SPCK, 2021) and other books and resources, including her guide for small groups, *The Prayers of Jesus* (Waverley Abbey Resources, 2020). She enjoys running the Woman Alive book club and speaking at churches. Find her at amyboucherpye.com

Naomi Aidoo

Naomi Aidoo is the Founder of *Time & Pace*, where she helps people go and grow towards their goals, making success sustainable. Previously, Naomi worked as a High School Teacher for 7 years. Naomi has been a regular contributor to Premier Radio's *Thought of the Day* and is a published contributing author in the book *Hope Rising 365* (SPCK, 2019). Naomi is also a certified Coach in the *5 Voices* leadership program with GiANT Worldwide. She lives in South London, England with her husband and her adventurous toddler. You can find her at timeandpace.com

Copyright © Waverley Abbey Resources 2022. Published by Waverley Abbey Resources. Waverley Abbey Resources is an operating name of CWR, Waverley Abbey House, Waverley Lane, Farnham, Surrey GU9 8EP, UK. Tel: 01252 784700 Email: mail@waverleyabbey.org
Registered Charity No. 294387. Registered Limited Company No. 1990308.
Front cover image: Adobe Stock Images
Concept development, editing, design and production by Waverley Abbey Resources. Printed in England by Yeomans.

Revelation

AMY BOUCHER PYE

Welcome to our month in the book of Revelation! Are you sitting comfortably? Oh dear, I hear you sigh. Perhaps you're wondering about the eye-covered creatures with wings or the great beast or the horsemen of the apocalypse. Yes, we'll contend with some strange images, but we'll also find jewels, fine linen and living water in the new Jerusalem where we'll live with God for ever.

It helps to place this book into the context of its first readers, those in the early church. And to remember that Revelation is the New Testament book that draws most on the Old Testament, especially the books of Ezekiel and Daniel. The first readers would have been steeped in these writings and their genre of apocalyptic literature. Revelation means apocalypse, but not in a horror-story sense of natural disasters. Rather, here it entails the visions and revelations God gave to a prayerful person – John, who some commentators think was the beloved disciple, and some don't.

God through His Spirit brings this book alive for us today, just as He did for the original readers. In the early chapters we'll delve into the seven letters of Jesus and then we'll move to the revelations given to John. We'll learn of God's judgments against those who refuse to bend their knee to Him, but will also find His invitation to drink the water that will satisfy our thirst. I hope you enjoy the journey!

To help me understand Revelation and its symbolism I've leaned on several commentaries, especially *Revelation for Everyone* by Tom Wright and *NIV Application Commentary: Revelation* by Craig Keener.

Revelation 1:1–8

'The revelation from Jesus Christ, which God gave him to show... what must soon take place.' (v1)

For Prayer and reflection

Lord Jesus, the first and the last, the Alpha and Omega – lead me through Your revelation this month, that I might understand You better and love You even more. Amen.

Shining **brilliance**

Revelation 1:9–20

'I was in the Spirit, and I heard behind me a loud voice... which said: "Write"' (vv10–11)

E xiled to Patmos, a rocky, inhospitable Greek island, John may have despaired. He was probably held there as a prisoner for speaking out about Christ. But in that stark environment God revealed to him not only Jesus' letters to seven churches (with seven representing a perfect number, and thus the letters being symbolically addressed to all the churches) but a vision of the age to come. A place of exile becomes for him a rich space of communion with God 'in the Spirit' (v10).

And the focus is Jesus, as we see in John's description of one who appears in glorious colours and images – glowing bronze, blazing fire, brilliant as the sun. This is not the Jesus of the pastel pictures, but the man who is God and at whose feet John immediately falls, 'as though dead' (v17). Of course, Jesus is tender and merciful, and we can relate to Him as one who cares for our needs and loves us deeply. But our intimacy with Jesus shouldn't dilute our wonder at His majesty, glory, power and might. All creation worships Him, He who is united with the Father.

We might think that Jesus won't break through to us with a revelation – and of course neither you nor I will receive from Him a vision like that which He gave to John, which became part of Holy Scripture – but Jesus is the risen Christ, alive and at work in our world, as much as He was in the days of the early church. We can wait with expectancy for how He will reveal Himself to us – right here, right now.

Why not take some time sharing with Jesus how you want to honour Him for His majesty, and also ask Him to show Himself to you today?

For Prayer and reflection

Jesus, Lord of lords, You are good and true; You are loving and kind; You are the King of all kings. I worship and adore You. Amen.

First **love**

Theologian Tom Wright visited Ephesus, in western Turkey, and shares how he felt the grandeur of the city, walking among many of its first-century buildings and the graveyard for the gladiators. Yet he reflected how poignant it was not to find a single Christian church there. Those in Ephesus when John was in Patmos would have found this unbelievable. nfortunately, however, it's a fulfilment of the prophecy of Jesus in this letter to them: 'If you do not repent, I will come to you and remove your lampstand from its place' (v5). The lampstand, which appeared in Revelation 1, signified one of the seven churches.

Before issuing His warning, Jesus had good things to say to those in this bustling city; they worked hard for Him and endured hardships without growing weary (vv2–3). But He admonished them for giving up on their first love: 'Consider how far you have fallen!' (v5) What sadness Jesus must have felt when their ardour had cooled and His words of rebuke were fulfilled.

When we first come to faith in Christ, we often experience a honeymoon period, perhaps including amazing answers to prayer and other stunning spiritual experiences. But God may start to withdraw these types of experiences if we lean on them more than on Him; if we look more to the gift than to the giver. In the dry times we may experience, we can ask God to help us exercise faith even then, believing in His goodness and love when we don't feel those gifts at that moment. Through the Holy Spirit, He will strengthen our ability to believe and trust in Him. He loves to answer these kinds of prayers.

'Yet I hold this against you: you have forsaken the love you had at first.' (v4).

For Prayer and reflection

Loving God, help me never to lose my love for and commitment to You. When I start to turn away from You, draw me back and strengthen my faith in You. Amen.

About to **suffer**

**Revelation
2:8–11**

'Do not be afraid of
what you are about
to suffer.' (v10)

'Shore up your defences.' That's the word one of my trusted prayer intercessors had for me some years ago, and it rather filled me with dread. Would I enter a testing time, maybe, and therefore need to lean on more prayer intercessors? She assured me she didn't sense anything sinister approaching, but that God wanted to bless me. I did enter a time of testing, but it was one of blessing too as I felt held through her prayers, and those of others I gathered. I felt more able to move through the challenges because I knew a group of people were praying for me.

Jesus writes to the church in Smyrna with a message that may have filled them with dread – that they would suffer persecution and testing. Yet He starts by saying that He sees what they are going through: 'I know your afflictions and your poverty' (v9). Knowing that we're not overlooked by God can bring us comfort and strength. Yet they were about to suffer even more, partly because of the influence of those claiming to be Jewish who instead were part of a 'synagogue of Satan'; 'even to the point of death' (v10). He ends with the encouragement that a second death wouldn't hurt those who are victorious (v11), so they should remain faithful.

We shy away today from addressing suffering in the wealthy west, but many Christians around the world undergo daily persecution. Do you know of any Christians exiled from their home country who you could pray for or support practically? If not, why not spend some time praying for Christians in countries such as North Korea, the Yemen or Iran, that God would be near to them and help them.

**For Prayer
and reflection**

**Lord Jesus, we shy
away from
suffering. But You
said that in this
world we would
have trouble. Give
me the strength to
bear what I face
and renew my
hope in You. Amen.**

Fresh ways to engage your small groups

Are you looking for new ideas for your small groups?

Why not shake up the cycle with something different?

Andy Peck has three insightful seminars to get your small groups thinking. Try:

Renewing your Mind
Discover how the Bible's view of the mind overlaps with neuroscience

Understanding the Bible in today's world
Learn tools for wise interpretation and application

Building community through small groups
Develop biblical community with godly leadership

Andy's visiting churches all over the UK with these seminars. If you'd like him to come to you, please get in touch at **wvly.org/contact-us**

Weekend

Keeping pure

....

Revelation 2:12–17

'Nevertheless, I have a few things against you' (v14)

❝ t's easier to ask for forgiveness than permission.' Have you heard that tongue-in-cheek saying? People sometimes employ it when they go ahead with some action that they know they really shouldn't pursue. When we apply this type of thinking to our lives in Christ, we lean too heavily on God's grace and forgiveness rather than on serving Him wholeheartedly and obeying His teaching.

The church in Pergamum fell foul of a bit of this kind of thinking. They lived in a tough place of alternative gods and their idols, with Satan on the throne (v13). Although they followed Jesus, some of them adapted their beliefs in Christ to fit the ways of their world –as did the Israelites who were enticed to commit sexual and spiritual sin (v14). Jesus warned them to repent and to stay pure in their faith.

How might you have accommodated the beliefs of the culture you live in? Ask God to show you this weekend if and where you might need to repent and return to Him. That's a prayer He loves to answer as He draws us closer to Himself.

....

Optional further reading

Revelation: 7 Messages Received by Selwyn Hughes is a short and readable look at Jesus' letters to the churches.

True **holiness**

As you read these letters of Jesus to the churches, have you noticed the similar format of each thus far? Jesus describes Himself and then starts off by affirming the good in the churches: what they are doing right and how they hold true to their faith in Him. Then He lists the ways they have strayed from His teaching as He calls them back to full obedience. He ends the letter with an affirmation of what He gives to those who follow Him.

We read in this letter to Thyatira strong words to those who have been swayed by Jezebel (a name given to one reminiscent of Jezebel in 1 Kings, she who tormented the prophet Elijah). God's people need to notice Jesus' blazing eyes (v18) because He doesn't tolerate ungodliness; instead He seeks that His people desire to be holy. Jesus has strong words for Jezebel and those who follow her – they will 'suffer intensely' and she will lie on a 'bed of suffering' while her children will be struck dead (vv22–23).

Holiness has gone a bit out of fashion these days. Say the word to someone who isn't a Christian and they may describe a caricature of a street preacher or zealot. But even those who follow Christ may squirm at the thought of falling short of what we perceive as God's exacting standards. Yet as we give ourselves to Him more day by day, asking Him to fill us with His love and to grow within us the fruit of the Spirit, He delights to respond. We may not notice how we're changing, but others around us will – they'll see how we're more loving and kind; how we're concerned for their needs; how we hold our tongue when exasperated. May it be so!

Revelation 2:18–29

'Then all the churches will know that I am he who searches hearts and minds' (v23)

For Prayer and reflection

Jesus, You are holy and You poured out Your blood to wash away my sins. Create in me a clean heart, that I might serve You with joy and full commitment. Amen.

Remember and repent

Revelation 3:1–6

'I know your deeds; you have a reputation of being alive, but you are dead. Wake up!' (vv1–2)

When my son was young, he had a squint in one of his eyes and had to wear a patch on the other one for a few hours each day. At times I found it hard to see his cute little face partially covered up, but I knew that the strong eye would take over the weak eye if we didn't. That's what happened to a friend, who eventually lost sight in the weak eye.

To the church at Sardis Jesus writes, 'Strengthen what remains and is about to die' because although they have a reputation for being lively and vibrant, yet they 'are dead' (v2). They need to wake up and finish the good work that they started earlier. Or they, like those with a squint, will lose part of their vision.

Note how Jesus tells them to remember and then repent (v3). We too can take this admonition to heart. As we call to mind God's mercy and grace in our lives – through specific memories of how He's carried us through – we can feel our hearts turning tender as we feel sorrow for the ways we've failed such a loving and forgiving God. And when our hearts are clean before God, we needn't fear Him coming 'like a thief in the night' (1 Thess. 5:2) for our hearts won't condemn us.

Jesus also calls out those who haven't 'soiled their clothes' (v4), a wonderfully visual way for us to think about the purity that He gives us as He washes us clean. Those who walk with Jesus will live forever – they'll never have their names blotted out of the book of life.

Look back over the past week, or month, or year, with gratitude and – as needed – repentance. As Jesus says, 'Whoever has ears, let them hear what the Spirit says' (v6).

For Prayer and reflection

Loving Lord, help me to repent from the ways that I fail You and others. I want to be clothed in white, my name listed in the book of life. Amen.

Open door

**Revelation
3:7–13**

'What he opens no
one can shut, and
what he shuts no
one can open.' (v7)

Four of us women pray for each other regularly, and for a period of about six months we sensed God leading us to an image of open and closed doors. We each longed for breakthroughs and open doors in one way or another; such as in the lives of our loved ones, for our living and work situations, and so on. On a holiday in France one of us took photograph after photograph of stately and interesting doors – each a reminder that God through Jesus would open and shut the doors in His time and in His way. At times, we encouraged one another when some doors that we thought would open remained fully shut. With the help of God and each other, we could wait for the right doors to open.

Jesus writes without condemnation to those in Philadelphia, promising to open and shut the doors for them. Although they aren't strong, yet they've remained firm in their faith – even in the presence of the 'synagogue of Satan' (v9). They've endured with patience and will be spared the coming tribulation. Encouraging them to hold on to their faith (v11), Jesus promises that they'll be a pillar in God's temple (v12). The Temple in the Old Testament was the place where God's Spirit dwelled among His people, and God was promising that He was building a new temple as He filled them with His Spirit and that they'd dwell with Jesus forever.

What doors are opening for you? Which are closed, and how do you feel about that? You could search online for images of doors and use them as a visual aid to pray through the issues in your life that you'd like Jesus to intervene with. He's the open door.

**For Prayer
and reflection**

Lord God, please give me strength to wait when the doors close in front of me, and the courage to walk through those that open. I want to follow You. Amen.

Neither hot nor cold

**Revelation
3:14–22**

'Those whom I love
I rebuke and
discipline. So be
earnest and
repent.' (v19)

Reading through Jesus' final letter to the seventh church, we're left in no doubt how disappointed He is with them. He's about to spit them out of his mouth (v16) and they are 'wretched, pitiful, poor, blind and naked' (v17). Why? Because they are as lukewarm as the water that flows from their springs. He'd rather they be hot, fully on fire with love for Him, or cold, closed off to His grace, truth and transformation.

Laodicea was a thriving commercial centre, known especially for its cloth and eye treatments. Because its people were so self-sufficient, they became complacent about their faith; they leaned on their own strength instead of looking to God. They thought they were rich and didn't need a thing (v17), but their wealth had hoodwinked them regarding their real need for a Saviour. They were naked and ashamed, needing God's robes; they were blinded and needed God's salve for their eyes (v18).

Jesus assures them that He is the Amen (v14), which in the Hebrew Scriptures was an assurance that He'd follow through on His promises. Because He loves them so much He yearns that they would return to Him, and that's why He's sending them this rebuke (v19). He waits at that door – yes, with the handle on the inside, as Holman Hunt painted it in 'The Light of the World' (which hangs in St Paul's Cathedral, London) – and knocks.

Take a few moments to review the seven letters. Which one spoke to you most clearly, and why? Which shocked or rebuked you? Share your responses with God, asking Him to help you to sift through your reactions. Seek that He'll make you more like Jesus.

**For Prayer
and reflection**

Lord Jesus, I don't
want to be one that
You'd want to spit
out of Your mouth.
Fill me with love
for You, that I
might serve You
and love my
neighbour. Amen.

Heaven's throne

**Revelation
4:1–11**

"'Holy, holy, holy is
the Lord God
Almighty, who was,
and is, and is to
come.'" (v8)

Some years ago I was at a conference and we entered into a time of amazing worship of God. I've never experienced anything like it before or since; I felt that a cloud of grace enveloped us and God revealed Himself to us in special ways. More than one of us who had suffered miscarriages had a picture of our babies with Jesus. For a few moments, we had the sense of a veil being removed as we enjoyed a tiny glimpse of unseen reality.

John had much more than a small revelation; here, Jesus welcomes him into the throne room of heaven! There, he sees the one who shines like precious stones, surrounded by an emerald rainbow (v3) and 24 elders (v4) (who probably represent the 12 tribes of Israel and the 12 apostles). John experiences a feast for the senses, including winged creatures covered in eyes, and peals of thunder and flashes of lightning.

The crescendo of it all is the praise and worship of the true and living God. The winged creatures forever praise God with cries of holy three times over, while the elders humbly declare how worthy God is to receive 'glory and honour and power', for He has created all things.

Worshiping God is why we were made; it's our main purpose and privilege. It's what sets us apart from the animals, as intelligent as many of them are. Without coercion we can bow before our creator and give Him all of the worship and praise, which He gladly receives.

This chapter and the next have been called the greatest in the Bible. It's worth spending some time immersing ourselves in their glorious words and images.

**For Prayer
and reflection**

Holy, holy, holy
are you, Lord. You
are He who was,
and who is, and
who is to come. All
praise and glory to
You! Amen.

Learn to be the Difference

You'll find space to learn and grow alongside a strong Christian heritage.

Waverley Abbey College provides training that ranges from one day seminars up to five-year part-time Higher Education courses, within three faculties:

- Counselling
- Theology
- Leadership

"It was a brilliant experience; the peaceful and positive atmosphere at Waverley; the friendships formed; the supportive tutors; the course material; the practical work and the encouragement."

- David Cunliffe, graduate

To find out more about any of our courses, check out our website. Or come and visit us for an open day. Register your interest here:

wvly.org/open-days

Learn to be the Difference

Introduction to Christian Care and Counselling

This five-day course introduces you to the practical methods and theory in counselling and pastoral care.

Whether or not you work in a pastoral setting, this course teaches you invaluable skills to support those around you.

Our next courses begin on:

- Farnham Campus: 27 June 2022
- Bradford Campus: 21 June 2022

Find out more and register your interest at:
wvly.org/iccc

The many sevens

....

Revelation 5:1–14

'To him who sits on the throne and to the Lamb be praise and honour and glory and power' (v13)

As we step into the rich imagery of the throne room, we find ourselves immersed in sometimes confusing images in the coming chapters. In his commentary, Tom Wright helpfully sets out what the various series of seven things mean. It's useful to share his wisdom as we enter into the prophecies so that we can have a sense of what's to come.

We've seen the seven letters of Jesus, which then introduce what comes next: the seven seals that must be broken in order for God's scroll to be unrolled (in chapters 6:1–8:1). The seventh seal then introduces seven trumpets, which are blown one by one (in chapters 8:6–11:15). After this, we encounter the sources of evil (chapters 12–15), which lead to the final sequence of seven: the bowls of God's wrath and how God uses them to defeat evil (chapters 15–20). We then come to the final joyful unveiling of the New Jerusalem where we'll live with God for ever.

It's a lot to take in, but it all centres around the Lion who is the Lamb – He who was slain for us that we might join all the creatures in heaven and on earth in unceasing praise.

....

Optional further reading

Tom Wright's commentary makes what can feel like tough passages of text easier to understand, in *Revelation for Everyone*. (SPCK, 2014)

Horse and **rider**

Revelation 6:1–17

'Its rider was given power to take peace from the earth and to make people kill each other.' (v4)

A year ago I was in a lot of pain from an arthritic hip. I'd ache when I walked too far and I found sleeping difficult. If one of our kids jostled me just the wrong way, I'd yelp in pain. Getting the hip replaced was major surgery, and I found it humbling to walk slowly with crutches as I recovered. But cutting out all that was rotten did the trick and now I'm mostly pain-free – and so very grateful.

We enter into some tough chapters in John's revelation. Things seem to get much worse before they're better, and we might wonder why God allows and even empowers the riders of these horses to wreak havoc and destruction. On a much, much larger scale, He's allowing the rotten flesh to fester so that He can cut it all out at once. The riders have only the power *given* to them – but that power involves more death and destruction. And even more martyrdom of the saints.

When this appears puzzling, something to keep in mind as we move forward into the series of sevens again comes from Tom Wright; namely that these successive seals and trumpets and bowls probably aren't meant to be understood sequentially but rather as happening at the same time. Thus, as God brings forward in the earth all of the rotten bits at once, He's able to – through His Son Jesus, the Lion and the Lamb – rid the world of all that opposes Him. We'll get there at the end of the book, but until then we have a lot of hanging on to do.

How do you feel about God empowering the rider to 'kill by sword, famine and plague, and by the wild beasts of the earth' (v8)? How can you reconcile this as falling within His bigger purposes?

For Prayer and reflection

Creator God, You know what's best for me in all things. I don't pretend to understand why suffering happens and why You allow it, but I will trust in You. Amen.

The **great** multitude

**Revelation
7:9–17**

'Salvation belongs
to our God, who
sits on the throne,
and to the Lamb.'
(v10)

As I walked around our local park in North London, I heard a smattering of languages and recalled a friend rueing the lack of people speaking English in the park. His comments had surprised me, and I wondered if he remembered that he could question *my* right to be there as much as theirs, as an American who had made her home in Britain. In contrast, I enjoy hearing the different accents and languages, and wonder what it was like before God limited our ability to understand each other (see Genesis 11). Indeed, how glorious it will be in the new kingdom of heaven, when the great multitude who stand before the throne are too numerous to count. They'll come from every tribe and people group, and speak every language (v9).

As we see in this passage, they will don white robes and hold palm branches, which probably hint to prophecy in the Old Testament, such as the vision of the end times given to Daniel. Daniel learned that people would be 'be purified, made spotless and refined' (Dan. 12:10) and thus could wear the white robes that signify purity. The palm branches could refer to the Feast of Tabernacles, which celebrated God's people's exodus from Egypt. And the branches could also point to those that welcomed Jesus into Jerusalem on Palm Sunday. God weaves His story throughout the generations.

Note, too, the cleansing and uniting work of the Lamb who is also their shepherd (v17), who will lead them to refreshing water (as David expressed in Psalm 23). And in some truly comforting words, we learn that 'God will wipe away every tear from their eyes' (v17). Lord, may it be so.

**For Prayer
and reflection**

Lord, give me
courage and
strength to
continue faithfully
until I meet You
face to face. All
glory and honour
belongs to You.
Amen.

The seven **trumpets**

magine if you were there with John as the veil between heaven and earth lifted. Consider the sounds coming to you from all angles as the winged creatures and the 24 elders praised God continually. And then, in a moment, *all fell silent.* For a long half-hour.

The silence would have captured everyone's attention, alerting them that something important was coming. They would have been expectant, perhaps filled with dread when they saw the trumpets being passed round to the seven angels. In the Old Testament, trumpets were often used to sound an alarm (see Joel 2:1 or Amos 2:2).

But before the trumpets, an angel is given a censer (a container in which to burn incense) which represents the prayers of God's people. God answers the cries for vindication, help and judgment, for after the prayers and incense are released come 'peals of thunder, rumblings, flashes of lightning and an earthquake' (v5). For reasons we don't fully understand, God welcomes and honours our prayers. And although He may not answer our cries as soon as we reach out to Him, He will, as we see here, eventually put everything right.

And then come the seven trumpets. With each sounding, plagues of hail, blood and fire are released, each bringing destruction in its wake (reminiscent of the plagues in Exodus). We may recoil at the thought of judgment, but the early Christians, suffering persecution under Roman rule, probably found comfort and encouragement from seeing that evil will one day be silenced.

Why not spend some time today crying out to God for all those who are persecuted for their faith.

'When he opened the seventh seal, there was silence in heaven for about half an hour.' (v1)

For Prayer and reflection

Father God, strengthen those who aren't allowed to worship You; those who could be killed for honouring You. Give them hope and carry them through, day by day. Amen.

Sweet then **sour**

**Revelation
10:1–11**

'It tasted as sweet
as honey in my
mouth, but when I
had eaten it, my
stomach turned
sour.' (v10)

B efore the seventh angel blows the seventh
trumpet, we enter an interlude when a mighty
angel arrives decked in symbolism that echoes
earlier chapters of Revelation. The imagery points to
him speaking on behalf of God and, when he shouts, it
sounds like thunder. But note that a voice from heaven
stops John from recording what he saw (v4). We don't
know why he was restrained, but perhaps it's a reminder
that God is God and we are His limited creatures who
do not need to know everything; indeed, who cannot
comprehend everything.

Then the angel opens a little scroll, which many
scholars think represents the book of Revelation. John
is instructed to take and eat it, and although it will taste
sweet in his mouth, it will turn sour in his stomach. The
Bible refers to God's words as sweeter than honey
(see Psa. 19:10 and 119:103) but here the early readers
probably would have thought of Ezekiel. This prophet
was called to speak to a rebellious nation, God's
own people in exile. In preparation for his task, God
instructed him to 'eat this scroll' of words of lament that
would taste sweet as honey. Ezekiel was faithful to his
task but faced opposition (Ezek. 2–3). John, too, was
to eat the scroll and proclaim its challenging message.
And this time the audience was not limited only to the
Israelites.

We don't know when the end times will come, but this
passage can encourage us to 'eat the scroll' of the Bible
in order to be ready, meditating on its words so that they
go deep within. Then we will be able to speak the sweet
words at just the right moment.

**For Prayer
and reflection**

**Lord, help me to be
so soaked in Your
love that if I am
called to deliver a
tough message I
can do so with
grace and
affirmation. Amen.**

Saving words

**Revelation
12:7–17**

'They triumphed
over him by the
blood of the Lamb
and by the word of
their testimony'
(v11)

W hen we read stories of people who are
martyred for their faith, we may wonder how
we'd react if we were in their place. Would
we stand strong and affirm our love for God when faced
with certain death via a knife or a gun? I pray we'll never
find out.

In this part of John's revelation we see the power of
the faithfulness of the saints. As the curtain continues to
be drawn back, it reveals the great drama taking place
in the heavenlies. There is war in heaven, with Michael
and his troops fighting against the dragon – that is,
Satan – and his dark angels. How was this victory
brought about? Satan was defeated in his evil mission
not only by Jesus' death on the cross but by the 'word
of their testimony'. God triumphs over the evil one – he
who accuses the saints continually – through those who
'did not love their lives so much as to shrink from death'
(v11).

What an amazing thought, that we collaborate
with God through our lives and witness and can stand
against the schemes of the evil one, in whatever guise
they appear. As we share with others how God works
in our day-to-day lives, we can spread hope and
encouragement to those who may wonder if God is real
or still active in the world. This passage reminds us not
to underestimate the power of our testimony, however
humble or ordinary it may appear to us.

Consider taking some time to write out the story of
your life with God, perhaps starting by noting key events
and happenings in bullet points. How do you see God's
love and mercy working in and through you? With whom
could you share your story?

**For Prayer
and reflection**

**Creator Lord, how
amazing that You
work through me
and my story!
Enlarge my vision,
that I might
partner with You in
sharing Your love
and light in the
world. Amen.**

Weekend

Following the Lamb

....

Revelation 14:1–5

'They follow the Lamb wherever he goes.' (v4)

I n contrast to the beasts who appear in Revelation 13, in this chapter we move to Mount Zion, the place of God's people, the new Jerusalem. Remember how much of Revelation is rooted in Old Testament imagery? Here we can look to Psalm 2, where the nations conspire and the kings of the earth rise up (Psalm 2:1–2) but the 'One enthroned in heaven... scoffs at them' (v4) because He has 'installed my king on Zion, my holy mountain' (v6). Those in power on the earth can't compete against the Lord or His anointed one.

With God are the 144,000 followers who have God's names on their foreheads: a symbolic number depicting the faithful believers. This elite group lives with purity and truth. They never lie nor defile themselves because they follow the Lamb wherever He goes (v4).

Amid the images of scary beasts and monsters in an unforgiving sea, John receives a flash of hope as he glimpses those who stay true to God. This weekend, think of several friends who have inspired you in your faith. How do they worship Jesus, and how can you follow their example in doing so?

....

Optional further reading

Read and pray through Psalm 2, perhaps in the Amplified Bible or something different.

God's **harvest**

**Revelation
14:6–20**

'The angel...
gathered its grapes
and threw them
into the great
winepress of God's
wrath.' (v19)

A few years ago I was surprised to hear the conversion story of an avowed atheist academic. What surprised me was not that she became a believer in Jesus, but that she did so through the arguments about the existence of hell. She read theologians such as Tom Wright and prominent thinkers such as C.S. Lewis as she examined the evidence for the validity of the gospel. Convinced, she turned from her atheism and believed.

Many people today don't believe in hell or demons, and the preaching of fire and brimstone is not common anymore. After all, talking about grapes being gathered up and thrown into the winepress, which then results in blood rising as high as the horses' bridles, doesn't exactly make for polite conversation. I'm not advocating this approach! But sometimes people are swayed to examine the reality of ultimate things such as heaven and hell. And in the Scriptures we will find the tools to aid them in their search.

Each generation seems to lean one way or another when it comes to sharing our faith in God. In previous times, fiery preaching warning listeners to avoid hell was common; people might have shared images such as the wrath of God poured at full strength into His cup or those who worship the beast being 'tormented with burning sulphur' (v10). Today, however, we more commonly emphasise the love of God; that He doesn't seek to scare us into following Him but welcomes us lovingly and without any manipulation. Yet have we veered too far over to this side, withholding discussion of the judgment of God who gave His only Son to die in order that we might live? I fear so.

**For Prayer
and reflection**

Lord, inspire me
with just the right
words as I share
how You have
worked in my life.
Help me to have
courage to speak
the truth but to do
so with love. Amen.

The seven **bowls**

Revelation 16:1–21

'They cursed the name of God... but they refused to repent and glorify him.' (v9)

We hear of deathbed conversions, the moments of grace where the one facing death becomes sweet as they seek forgiveness from God and their loved ones. Perhaps those stories stand out because the alternative is striking – someone so entrenched in their ways that they can't or won't change. I wonder how much more likely is this latter behaviour than the amazing stories of grace. God can and does intervene, but He also respects the decisions that people make.

The sad fact is that many people choose not to repent and, in the third series of sevens in John's revelation, we see God's seven bowls of wrath being poured out in judgment against those who will not bend their knee to Him. Again the plagues of Egypt are invoked in the images of blood, sores and fire that are poured out of the bowls, and again the early church would have thought back to God's protection of His people against their oppressors.

Throughout the description of what the seven bowls unleash, we find a line repeated: 'they refused to repent'. And there's a similar sentiment in verse 21: 'they cursed God'. Those who worship the beast have become hardened in their beliefs, and though they have a chance to turn from their sins and turn to God, they don't. Instead, they curse God and die.

In the light of this stark judgment, this passage serves as a reminder to keep our hearts supple before God, coming to Him in repentance for our wrongdoing and receiving from Him the forgiveness for our sins. Our lifetime of habits can result not in a hardened heart, but in a countenance of worship and gratitude.

For Prayer and reflection

Lord, keep my heart soft. I know I can so easily dig in and get stuck in my own way of thinking. Give me a glimpse of Your holiness; I want to glorify You. Amen.

The **fall** of Babylon

'Come, I will show you the punishment of the great prostitute, who sits by many waters.' (v1)

Over the past years people seem to be increasingly aware of the plight of those sold into sex slavery. Whereas previously onlookers perhaps thought that many chose this way of life, now the sad reality has come to light – of the driving needs of poverty, or drug addiction, which lead people into selling their bodies.

Thus when we read this section of Revelation, we should again remember that John employs symbolic language and looks back to the Old Testament. The image of God's people committing spiritual adultery was prominent in the Hebrew Scriptures, so it's not surprising that Babylon, the enemy of God's people, is pictured as a prostitute. She's glittery on the outside, decked out with expensive jewellery, but she stinks from within. Her goblet contains 'abominable things and the filth of her adulteries' (v4) – picture a cup filled with bodily fluids and secretions. I'm sorry for dwelling on this, but we can easily miss what an 'abomination' actually looks like.

In the story of Hosea, God called him to marry Gomer, a prostitute who would continue to betray him (Hosea 1:2–3). The original readers would have remembered his story and how it revealed God's heart for His people. Again and again they left Him as they hankered after other gods. Again and again He welcomed them back. But He didn't do so without it costing Him dearly.

The sins that we brush off as minor or not troubling could be the ones that lead us to the next turning from God. We can ask God through His Holy Spirit to keep our hearts pliable as we confess our wrongdoings regularly and receive His loving forgiveness.

For Prayer and reflection

Loving God, how much it must hurt You when Your people worship other things. Help me to look to You to fill my needs and to purify my heart. Amen.

The wedding of the **Lamb**

**Revelation
19:1–10**

'For the wedding of
the Lamb has
come, and his
bride has made
herself ready.' (v7)

Phew! We've made it through the seven trumpets and seven bowls of woe, along with the crushing of Babylon. It's not been an easy journey, but I hope that makes it all the more sweet as we land on the wedding of the Lamb and His Bride. We rejoice because the evil one has been defeated, the Lord God reigns and the Church prepares to become the Bride, united with her Bridegroom for all eternity. Hallelujah!

Notice that word, 'hallelujah', which means 'praise God'. It appears so often in the Psalms that I was surprised to learn from a commentary that it only appears in the New Testament here in this chapter. The use of the word builds with each of the four exclamations: 'Hallelujah, salvation belongs to our God' (v1); 'Hallelujah! The smoke from her goes up for ever and ever' (v3) – the whore will never again rear her head.– it is finished'; 'Hallelujah, praise God all you who fear Him!' (v5); and finally, 'Hallelujah, the wedding of the Lamb has come' (v7). This is what we've been waiting for. The bride makes herself ready, donning the fine linen that points to the white robes put on by the martyrs (Rev. 6:11). But note that the fine linen stands for all of the righteous acts of God's people, and not just those who died for their faith.

**For Prayer
and reflection**

Loving God, help
me to make myself
ready, putting on
Your fine linen
through my acts of
love and service.
Amen.

Last Friday, we saw how the Lord honours the testimony of His saints. Here, note in verse 10 how that testimony comes through the Holy Spirit. The angel reminds John that they are fellow created beings who God uses to spread His glory. Thus we should not give up hope, for the true and living God sees our faithful words and deeds.

The **return** of Jesus Christ

John introduces another vision, in which we meet the resurrected Jesus who returns as the conquering King. Again the language drips with symbolism and, although we might be put off by the militaristic language, remember that Jesus won the victory through His selfless death.

Some background on the various symbols can be helpful. Jesus rides in on a white horse, which would be appropriate for rulers as white horses were regarded as the best. His blazing eyes probably refer to Daniel's vision of the warrior in a great war with 'eyes like flaming torches' (Daniel 10:6). Jesus is the King, as symbolised by the many crowns, and His robe dipped in blood may refer either to His own blood shed on the cross or the blood of His opponents. The language echoes much of Isaiah 63, such as the red garments from trampling the winepress: 'their blood spattered my garments' (Isa. 63:3). The saints, in contrast, wear the fine linen, as mentioned previously.

As the vision unfolds, John sees an angel calling people to join in the great feast of God, and those poised against Jesus waging war on Him. Without seemingly much fuss – and without the drama we'd find in a science fiction film – Jesus throws the beast and the false prophet into the burning sulphur. Done. Jesus wins!

Spend some time pondering prayerfully our Saviour and Lord covered in these blood-stained garments while we receive clean and pure white linen to wear. Because of our shameful wrongdoing we don't deserve to don these clean clothes; we should be dressed more like Jesus. But He went to the cross that we could be made clean.

Revelation 19:11–21

'On his robe and on his thigh he has this name written: KING OF KINGS AND LORD OF LORDS.' (v16)

For Prayer and reflection

Conquering Lord, You have won the victory for me! Help me not to forget what this cost You. Make me ever grateful and help me to serve You all the more. Amen.

Final defeat

....

Revelation 20:1–15

'Then death and Hades were thrown into the lake of fire.' (v14)

For our final weekend together I invite you to a little light reading – not! Much ink has been spilled as Bible commentators seek to understand the thousand years of Satan being bound and then his rearing his very ugly head again. They discuss not only theories of premillennialism, amillennialism and postmillennialism (roughly, whether the thousand years means Jesus will establish a kingdom of His rule, or whether it's symbolically happening now, or will happen in the future) but the tribulation (what happened in Revelation 6–19).

I follow a different school of interpretation that focuses not so much on the thousand years and what it means but considers the importance of God making sure that all of the evil one's influence has been fully removed so that He can defeat him fully. God allows Satan to roam again in order that there's no question that he's been fully routed. All that remained was death and Hades, and God throws them into the lake of fire too (v14). At last, we enter the final joyous chapters where death and evil are defeated and we enjoy God's presence forever.

....

Optional further reading

Read Jesus' comforting words to His friends as He prepared them for life after He died in John 14–17.

More from your authors

Get 10% off titles by Amy Boucher Pye

7 Ways to Pray

Cover to Cover Lent Study
Guide: Prayers of Jesus

A **new** heaven and earth

**Revelation
21:1–8**

'He who was seated
on the throne said,
I am making
everything new!'
(v5)

I was deeply moved as I heard a friend describe a
visit to his mother in hospital, as she neared the end
of her life. He held her hand and tried to assure her
that all would be well, but only when he began to read
to her from the last chapters of Revelation did she find
peace. As he painted the picture of the new heavens
and the new earth, he could see her anxiety dissipate as
her breathing began to slow from her previous agitated
state. She squeezed his hand, and his eyes brimmed
with tears of sorrow and joy.

This peace reigns in John's vision, for the war is fully
and completely over and God dwells with His people
in a time of abundance (v3). This word 'dwell' here is
important; it refers to God making His dwelling in the
tabernacle in Exodus 36–40, and to John's Gospel,
where it implies that Jesus pitches His tent amongst us:
'The Word became flesh and made his dwelling among
us' (John 1:14).

Because the saints live for ever with Jesus, no longer
are they marked by tears and mourning, but joy as they
live in the new Eden. Their thirst is slaked by the water of
life, and all things are made new. All things!

Imagine a world without death or mourning or crying
or pain. As we hold this picture in our minds and hearts,
we can face hardship and sorrow, for we know God
welcomes us to inhabit this new heaven and new earth.
Amazingly, this isn't a glorious reality reserved only for
after we die, but God welcomes us to collaborate with
Him now in the ushering in of this kingdom here on earth.
His gifts of love and life aren't reserved only for later; He
wants us to enjoy them now.

**For Prayer
and reflection**

**Father, You are
making all things
new! Release me
from all that I cling
to that isn't of You,
so that You can use
me to welcome
others to life in
Your kingdom.
Amen.**

The **Holy** City

Revelation 21:9–21

'It shone with the glory of God, and its brilliance was like that of a very precious jewel' (v11)

One of the seven angels takes John 'in the Spirit' and shows him the Bride, the Holy City of Jerusalem. Glorious images of God's glory and how He dwells with His people come to John, as summed up so well by C.S. Lewis, in the final instalment of his Narnia tales, *The Last Battle*: 'The things that began to happen after that were so great and beautiful that I cannot write them. And for us this is the end of all the stories, and we can most truly say that they all lived happily ever after. But for them it was only the beginning of the real story...'

What John names are jewels and light, gold and jasper, and the glory of God. This Holy City is a gift from God that comes down from heaven. It shines with God's glory, which is so bright that no longer are the sun or moon needed. It's likened to a jewel, and 12 precious stones adorn the walls, which were the 12 stones represented on the high priest's breastplate, where each stone stood for one of the tribes of Israel (see Exodus 28:17–21). In the ancient world cities had walls, but the gates of this one will always be open, and there the 12 tribes of Israel are named, with the 12 apostles symbolised in the foundation stones.

What a glorious picture! God doesn't withhold from His people the finest in jewels or other natural resources, but makes them available for us to enjoy – even as He makes Himself fully available to us. This is not a picture of a tyrant taskmaster but one of a giving parent who loves us deeply. 'See what great love the Father has lavished on us, that we should be called children of God! And that is what we are!' (1 John 3:1).

The Last Battle by CS Lewis © copyright CS Lewis Pte Ltd 1956. Extract used with permission

For Prayer and reflection

Lord God, spark my imagination into life with images of Your love for me that I might live out of Your goodness and grace. Amen.

Seeing God

Revelation 21:22—22:5

'They will see his face, and his name will be on their foreheads.' (v4)

John glimpses the reality of God dwelling with His people. No longer is there a Temple, for the whole city is God's temple, His meeting place with His people where they live together for ever in peace, joy and abundance. There in the new heaven and the new earth; the redeemed will live with God and will see Him face to face. Their faces will radiate His glory, as Moses' face shone when, for 40 days, he received the Law while meeting with God on the mountain (Exod. 34:29–33). Moses had to put a veil over his face when he came down from the mountain, to hide this glory from the Israelites, but in the new world there will be no need for veils or hiding. All of God's people will radiate His glory.

This is the new Eden, and a river flows through the middle, even as a river watered the garden in Eden (Gen. 2:10). The trees produce healing leaves and fruit, and fulfil Ezekiel's prophecy of leaves that don't wither and fruit that doesn't fail (Ezek. 47:12). God's people will be nourished with His glorious and nutritious food.

When I consider trees that neither wither nor fail, I can't help but think of my grandparents on both sides, whose lives as farmers were marked with the daily toil of caring for the land and the animals. If they experienced drought or floods, they'd suffer until the new season came with its hope of new life. I wonder if we'll care for the vegetation in the Holy City. Think about gardening without the curse – even someone without a green thumb like me would grow lush and fragrant plants.

No more curse; no more night. This is life in the kingdom of God. May it be so!

For Prayer and reflection

God, I long to see You face to face! Meet me here and now in Your kingdom. Refresh me and fill me with hope and love for You. Amen.

Coming **soon**

'The Spirit and the bride say, "Come!" And let the one who hears say, "Come!"' (v17)

Wh at's the most amazing invitation you've ever received? Mine might be the last-minute invitation to celebrate American Thanksgiving at the US ambassador's residence in London. My husband and I were a bit wowed to be in such august company and in such a grand setting.

But the invitation that forms the end of John's vision – and indeed our Bibles – tops anything any one of us has experienced thus far. For God welcomes us to join Him in the Holy City. When we wash our robes and put on our clean, white linen, we enter the gates of the only city that will never sleep. There we will enjoy our life with God, united with Him and with our sisters and brothers.

Notice the focus on Jesus and the many titles for Him that appear in these few lines. He's the Alpha and Omega, the First and Last, the Beginning and the End. He's the Root and the Offspring of David; the bright Morning Star. All things come from Him and are given through Him. He was there at the foundation of the world and is there in the city to come. He is the perfect offspring of David (Rev. 5:5), who was the ideal king in the Old Testament. As the Morning Star, Jesus is the fulfilment of the promise made in Revelation 2:28 and in Numbers 24:17: 'A star will come out of Jacob.'

We're welcomed to come and drink, in words that echo the glorious invitation in Isaiah 55:1: 'Come, all you who are thirsty, come to the waters; and you who have no money, come, buy and eat!'. Just as we are, we come, with gratitude and joy for how the Lord beckons us. We join John in saying, 'Come, Lord Jesus'.

For Prayer and reflection

Loving Lord, we worship You and give thanks for the way You love us. Help me to serve You without losing heart, for I know You love me unceasingly. Amen.

Reflective Routine and Radical Rest

Naomi Aidoo

Luke 5:12–16

'But Jesus often withdrew to lonely places and prayed.' (v16)

For Prayer and reflection

Lord, thank You for Your ultimate example of rest and retreat. I pray You'll show me how to follow in Your footsteps, especially in the in the midst of my busy daily life. Amen.

'm someone who very much likes to be in control and plan ahead. In fact, my parents have memories of me as a child asking what we were going to have for dinner whilst I was still eating lunch. It's no surprise then, that the concept of surrender, retreat and rest isn't one which I understood very well when I first seriously committed my life to the Lord.

The idea of radical rest can be a triggering one. We live in a world which tells us that in order to become more and to have more, we have to *do* more. As believers in Jesus we know that a lot of the time, the opposite is true and that, often, some of the most important work that we can do is actually to rest and retreat in order to more clearly hear the Father's heart. Although this is still not something which comes easy to me on a daily basis, it's something that I've spent my recent years learning the value and importance of more and more, every single day. Today's passage gives us a perfect model to follow in the attitude and example of Jesus.

He is at a point in His ministry where He's become increasingly well known, and people have come from far and wide to encounter Him. Yet despite their needs and this apparent pressure, we read that he would often withdraw to desolate places and pray.

I love this tangible example that Jesus provides us with – to rest in spite of the demands and to-do lists. Here, we also note what that rest will bring – time with the Father. This month, we'll be going on a journey together to seek Him in the midst of the busyness, and I for one am thankful that He's paved the way.

Give to make a difference

Our Bible reading notes are read by hundreds of thousands of people around the world. *Every Day with Jesus* and *Inspiring Women Every Day* are now free in the UK. We want everyone, whatever their financial means to have access to these resources that help them walk each day with our Saviour.

It makes all the difference. One reader in Malaysia said:

When I was first exposed to Every Day with Jesus about two years ago, I could sense something different, something refreshing, and I was energised. I used to struggle to translate knowledge into my daily life. EDWJ helped me to be more insightful, more positive, and to enjoy everyday life as a disciple. This helps me to be patient and positive at home, at work, and at church.

As we trust in God's provision, we know there are costs to providing this ministry. Can you give to make a difference in someone's life? Could supporting this vision be a way in which you serve?

A gift of just £2 a month from you will put daily Bible reading notes into the hands of at least one person who is hungry to know God and experience His presence every day.

Visit **wvly.org/donate** to give to make a difference, or use the form at the back of these notes.

Grit and gift

....

Psalm 103:13–16

'For he knows how we are formed, he remembers that we are dust.' (v14)

I t's funny, but I used to find our key verse today a little offensive. The idea that despite all of our gifts, complexities, achievements and abilities, the Lord still remembers us as 'dust'. Yet it's wonderful how, in reading the word numerous times, it can take on a fresh meaning with every encounter. I've very recently gone through a lot of change and uncertainty in my life; from career shifting, to a missed miscarriage at 12-weeks pregnant – all whilst parenting a two-year-old, which is ever unpredictable!

In the midst of feeling broken, tired, frustrated and overwhelmed, to name but a few of the emotions I've felt in the last few months, it's been a source of true comfort for me to know that the Lord remembers that I am dust.

Yes, we're gifted, talented and wonderfully unique people, each with our own personalities and quirks. But we're human beings – not human doings.

It was never our responsibility to hold the weight of the world, because our Lord and Saviour died in our place so that He could carry it. This isn't our weakness but rather His *gift*, and one I now longingly receive.

....

Optional further reading

Naomi Aidoo, *The Time Journal*®, 2021, timeandpace.com/thetimejournal

When the **work** never finishes

Genesis 2:1–3

'By the seventh day God had finished the work he had been doing; so on the seventh day he rested from all his work.' (v2)

Between running my business, supporting my husband with his company, keeping our house *relatively* clean and being a mum to an energetic two-year-old, it's safe to say that my to-do list never ends.

I can imagine that as you're reading this, you're nodding in agreement. You're busy. *Life* is busy. But what refreshment and challenge is the Lord presenting us with as we read of what He did in today's passage. Here, the creator of heaven and earth takes a break. It's safe to say that He wasn't done with His work – He's still working today, after all. But He was done for now.

Yes, we may have a laundry basket which appears to magically refill every time we reach the bottom. We may also have school runs, church commitments, full-time jobs or businesses, and everything else in between. But when we look at the example of the Father here, with the understanding that we're to follow His lead, that means resting – and not just grabbing a lukewarm cup of tea when we're presented with a moment to pause, but rather *intentional* and carved-out rest.

One of things I made space for in the framework I've created within my business, which is about work–life wellbeing, is to think about three main intentions of the day. The idea is that, even though there's always work to be done, ticking off just those three things gives me both a sense of accomplishment and a reason to pause. Sometimes pause needs to be practised before it can be integrated into our every day.

The Lord's work was flinging stars into space and breathing life into dust. Your work will look different, but your call to rest doesn't change.

For Prayer and reflection

Thank You, Father, that rest is not just a nice idea, but something You both demonstrated and call us to. Help me to be intentional and deliberate with rest. Amen.

The path of **purpose**

John 4:1–10,39–
42

'Now he had to go through Samaria.'
(v4)

They say hindsight is 20/20, and although I've found the reality of this relatively overused statement quite frustrating in the moment, I must say that there are a plethora of situations I can look back on and be grateful for the fact that they didn't work out the way I'd hoped.

I've always been struck by the use of the phrase 'had to' in our key verse today. After further study, I learned that the route Jesus took to get to Galilee wasn't most easily done via Samaria. Yet, that's what He did here. But why?

As we note in verse 42 of our passage, this seemingly chance (although not chance at all) encounter with the Lord by the Samaritan woman led to many in her town being saved. What may have at first seemed like a random and everyday occurrence had divine and destiny-driven implications.

As you go about your days, weeks and beyond, you may well be wondering what the significance of some of the seemingly purposeless tasks you undertake is. In a world which celebrates significance, strength and outward success, it can be tricky to feel purposeful and powerful when you're in the throes of everyday life – and, let's face it, more in 'survive' than 'thrive' mode.

Applying a little foresight to these situations can make a world of difference – at least, it helps me. Rather than feeling hard done by or forgotten about because of the mundanity of the moment, invite Jesus in and ask whether you 'having' to do this or go there now may well have eternal significance later. Then get ready to celebrate those moments of hindsight. He is able.

For Prayer and reflection

Have you ever, with hindsight, realised the reason for the random or even unwanted circumstances which have taken place in your life? How might that encourage you today?

Reasons and **seasons**

In 2016, after leaving teaching and embarking on making my part-time blog more of a business, I stumbled upon the personal development industry. Although a lot of what comes from that space might not be everyone's flavour, I certainly took to it like a duck to water.

I ran online communities of hundreds of women, filled courses and coaching programmes, went on radio, ran webinars, and quite honestly felt as though I was pursuing purpose and passion. Truth be told, I was, in part; but what I didn't account for was those seasons in life where we don't necessarily feel on top of the world.

After having my son and not immediately being able to work in the way I used to, I found myself wondering where the 'you've got this' motivation of my years of reading and investing in personal development had gone. I wondered whether I'd now somehow lost my ability to support people in the way I once did. I was pretty negative about myself because suddenly, without the morale-boosting motivation I'd once been accustomed to giving and receiving, I felt as though I'd somehow failed.

A quick look at our passage today reminds us that there is, in fact, 'a time for everything'. One season isn't necessarily worse than another. Sometimes, they're just different. I wish I'd given myself more grace in those moments of doubt and uncertainty, rather than forcing myself to be someone I no longer had the capacity or the desire to be.

Thankfully, the Lord meets us right where we are, whatever the season, and doesn't need to say 'you've got this' – because even when we haven't, He still has.

Ecclesiastes 3:1–8

'There is a time for everything, and a season for every activity under the heavens' (v1)

For Prayer and reflection

Lord, thank You so much for Your patience and loving care; for guiding and upholding me, no matter how I feel or what season of life I'm in. You hold it all. Amen.

Pressing into **purpose**

**Proverbs
31:10–31**

'She watches over
the affairs of her
household and
does not eat the
bread of idleness.'
(v27)

Although the infamous Proverbs 31 woman wasn't actually a real woman, but rather a fictional character created by a mother who was teaching her son the Hebrew alphabet, we can certainly learn a lot from her life (whilst simultaneously breathing a sigh of relief that this wasn't actually a woman who did *all* of that).

It's instilled within us from a young age that we will grow up and then proceed to go and do a job. At least, that's what it was like for me. School didn't teach me about entrepreneurship and so when I thought about my perceived limited options (which actually weren't limited at all), I swayed towards something which I felt was most suitable for my passions and abilities.

I was a teacher for seven years, and although I have many, many fond memories of the students I worked with and the friends for life I met there, I'm also reminded of the frequent frustration I'd feel at not doing *exactly* what I felt was right. Don't get me wrong, I didn't know what that thing was at the time, but I knew that there was something else for me.

**For Prayer
and reflection**

**Is there something
you've not pursued
for fear that it's not
the right thing?
How might the
example of the
Proverbs 31
woman encourage
you to step out in
faith today?**

Having since had seasons of full- and part-time church ministry, contracting for a big tech company and running my own business, it's been wonderful to recognise the diversity that our day to day can contain.

We are not 'one size fits all' and life isn't always linear. Although we're called not to be idle and lazy, there isn't a specific blueprint as to what that lack of laziness needs to look like. Don't label yourself in that way. Instead, go and grow towards the direction you're being called in. An exciting world awaits.

God's **will** over my when

'm sure I'm not alone in that, when I first came to faith, I interpreted today's key verse to mean that God was something like my personal genie. Thankfully, I was swiftly corrected, and then I recognised that what the verse actually means is something even better.

The more we walk in step with the Holy Spirit, the more our desires match up with the ones He planned for us before the beginning of time. When things aren't going the way I planned, I can certainly find myself getting irritable and frustrated. Not least when it seems as though everything is going right for everyone else but me.

Today's passage is a wonderful reminder and encouragement to me about trusting in His *will* over my *when*. I know that when I'm walking in step with His spirit and abiding in Him, I'm less focused on what it means to get my way in the way I want it.

Beyond this though, what always strikes me about this verse is not just our call to abide in the Lord, but to 'take delight' in Him. It got me thinking about what that tangibly looks like. Delighting in my husband, for example, might look like a toddler-free date night. Delighting in my son would probably look like a trip to feed the ducks followed by some ice cream on our favourite bench.

Delighting in the Lord has looked different for me at varying seasons of my life, but three absolute staples have been the Word, worship music and my journal. When I'm waiting for Him to show up in a season of my life which is stretching me, rather than impatiently tapping my feet I want to do my best to *delight* in Him.

Psalm 37:3–7

'Take delight in the LORD, and he will give you the desires of your heart.' (v4)

For Prayer and reflection

Lord, thank You that Your timing is perfect and Your way is secure. Help me not to look at the uncertainty around me but, instead, to delight in Your presence. Amen.

True triumph

....

Zechariah 9:9–13

'See, your king comes to you, righteous and victorious, lowly and riding on a donkey' (v9)

As we enter Palm Sunday this weekend, I find it striking to think about the juxtaposition of the meaning of triumph attached to Jesus' entry, alongside what this 'triumph' actually looked like in Him arriving on a donkey.

I was talking to my therapist recently about the battle I have with significance. The desire to 'make a mark' and do something which people celebrate and admire, comes alongside my desire to honour Jesus and ensure that I'm not allowing the ways of this world to skew my understanding of success.

But it's hard, isn't it?

Jesus' triumphant arrival in Jerusalem on a donkey gives us yet another beautiful example of His to follow, as we enter Holy Week this weekend.

In the midst of my battle to be seen to be doing well, I try now instead to think about the kingdom significance of the things done behind the scenes, the sacrifices in the silence, and the actions which look and sound like an arrival on a donkey might have – yet ones which my heavenly Father knows have far greater meaning.

....

Optional further reading
John 12:12–15

Daughter > disciple > doer

Today, as we continue through Holy Week, I want us to reflect on the magnitude of what the cross actually means. It means we're daughters. It means we're chosen by Him to follow Him. It means we have plans and purposes to walk out.

Sometimes, though, we get the order mixed up. We're ready to do what God has called us to do much quicker than we are to sit at His feet – because, you know, we're busy. But as we see in the life of Saul, we can fall as quickly as we can rise if we don't have our priorities straight.

Being called to pause isn't a popular message. Yet sometimes we get so swept up in the doing that we forget we're daughters first. Being a daughter means that your identity is found in Christ alone and not in your works or your status. Work is a *blessing*. But let's remember it can also be a distraction, a place where we build false idols and cling to being identified by something never promised to call us worthy.

So today, as we look to the cross, ask yourself how much of your doing stems from your identity as a daughter. Though the doing part is of huge importance, there's another D word of more significance: disciple. A disciple is one who is called-out; called to ^follow^ in obedience to Christ, always. Not to follow Him when it feels convenient or easy, or it's a Sunday. But to follow His commands in all things, always. Following is active, of course. You can't follow passively. But sometimes we *can* be active without the following part.

Today, let's remember that we are first chosen daughters of God, called to follow Him and *then* to walk in where He's leading us.

> **1 Samuel 18:1–16**
>
> 'Saul was afraid of David, because the LORD was with David but had departed from Saul.' (v12)

For Prayer and reflection

Is your doing shaped by what you've been called to do? Or what you feel as though you want to do? How do you typically tell the difference?

What's in it for **me**?

**Matthew
26:14–16**

'What are you
willing to give me
if I deliver him
over to you?' (v15)

W e'd be forgiven for having some real anger towards Judas as we read this account. 'How dare he?' might pop up in our minds. But the truth of the matter is, I've forsaken the Lord for a lot less than Judas' bag of silver was worth to him. I wonder if you can relate to the following:

- Doing X instead of listening to the still, small voice warning me against it.

- Blaming God (or at least giving Him the silent treatment) when things don't go my way.

- Deciding I know best.

Now, don't get me wrong. None of these are quite as drastic as the consequences that Judas' betrayal brought about, but my point here is that we can so often forget the bigger picture entirely as we think about betrayal and backstabbing in the Bible. The heart of both our dismissal and Judas' denial lies in the same question: 'What's in it for me?' It's not especially that we're out to get anyone else, it's just that our needs, comfort and desires have made it to the top of the list before thinking about the ramifications for anyone or anything else.

The good news is that the Lord sees and knows it all. He is gracious, patient and forgiving. But let's allow today's passage to also serve as a reminder. Before we ask why, or whether it's the best option for us, let's trust that wherever the Lord is leading us, it's for our good and His glory.

I think it's also important to note that Judas actively 'watched for an opportunity to hand him over' (v16). Instead of looking for opportunities to put our own selves first, let's find those which propel the purpose and needs of others.

**For Prayer
and reflection**

**Lord, please
forgive me for the
moments of
disobedience,
where I've stepped
outside of Your will.
Please help me to
do good to and for
others and not
only for myself.
Amen.**

Learning to **listen**

When I was 21 and had just recommitted my life to Jesus, I was *so* excited by my rekindled faith. I was on a gap year with my church at the time. With Bible studies daily, lessons in how to handle the Word, and opportunities to share what we'd been learning with one another and our pastor as a form of preaching practice, I was truly in my element. I look back on this much younger self with a huge sense of love, and a big smile, and whenever I read today's passage, I'm reminded of her.

Simon Peter was undoubtedly zealous for the Lord and thus ready and willing to act on whatever He suggested, let alone commanded. The moment Jesus washed the disciples' feet at the Last Supper was no exception.

Once the interaction and the understanding around the act had taken place between Jesus and Simon Peter, Jesus went on to teach that the most important thing to take away from this practical lesson of servanthood was to make it tangible, as opposed to theoretical.

Verse 17 has such an important lesson for us today. However, before we assume that this means our lives ought to look like endless to-do lists, then panic and push – let's pause.

My 21-year-old self had a heart after God but she didn't give herself much grace. She believed that if every single moment of her waking wasn't steeped in *doing*, she obviously wasn't serious about God.

Sometimes, our walk will look like doing. But at other times, our tangible obedience will look like *being* – keeping quiet for a moment, sitting at His feet and learning His will, as opposed to rushing ahead with what we *think* He's trying to say.

John 13:1–20

'Now that you know these things, you will be blessed if you do them.'
(v17)

For Prayer and reflection

Lord, thank You for Your example of servant leadership here, and also for Your reminder to listen first. Help us to know when is time to do, and when is time to be. Amen.

Passion

**Matthew
26:17–29**

'And while they
were eating, he
said, "Truly I tell
you, one of you will
betray me."' (v21)

Passion. It's what led every step and forced Jesus to continue when everything in Him wanted to turn back and quit. But quitting was never an option. Jesus was never going to take the easy road, to do what was convenient, to settle for satisfying self over surrendering to soul's call. Face like flint, He looked at those who were eagerly expecting greatness, at those who thought the whole suffering servant thing had been some kind of joke. There was nothing funny about that final dinner with the disciples. But there was passion. Passion enough to sit in suspense across from the one who essentially spat in His face. All the while knowing and not showing.

He spoke of betrayal but didn't point the finger. For what did a name matter now? This wasn't a sudden flurry of false humility and a desire to mark His martyrdom so that He could score higher on the suffering scale. This was just what it was – and passion kept Him.

'But God so loved...' (John 3:16) – a love like no other for the lost and the least. For me. For you. A love which didn't see a shortcut or a quick fix. A love which wanted to taste and see everything because this was the will of His father and it was good. At least, it was meant to be. But if there was ever a time to say that someone looked as though they were carrying the weight of the world on their shoulders, it was now. And He was.

Where has passion led you? When was the last time you were so persuaded by passion that it held you accountable to walking it out? Contrary to popular belief, it won't always be easy to follow passion.

But God.

**For Prayer
and reflection**

**Thank You, Lord,
for Your love and
passion for me;
that Your passion
paved a way that I
might live. Help me
to honour that
sacrifice with the
way I live and lead.
Amen.**

Nothing became **everything**

'The punishment that brought us peace was on him, and by his wounds we are healed.' (v5)

Good Friday – a Friday which, for the disciples who stuck around to watch their teacher, friend and Saviour hang from a cross like a common criminal, would have been utterly devastating.

'**Today is Friday. But Sunday's coming**' (emphasis added).* Yet whenever Good Friday comes around, I can't help but think about the disciples who watched on helplessly as everything they knew and trusted fell apart in front of their very eyes.

'But they knew the outcome', we might argue. And yet, how many times have *we* been promised something from God, only to doubt, second-guess and live up to our human-ness, stopping or quitting over believing Him at His word? What was promised no longer felt permanent for those disciples– as though all had been for nothing. Of course, the truth was anything but. The truth is what saved us, the truth is what continues to save us and the truth is good. Good for me and good for you. Without Him, *we're* nothing. Yet often, we choose actions which suggest that Jesus taking on our sins, and dying in our place that we might live, is what's considered nothing. Today may mark a time to be reflective, but Jesus' death, and indeed life, didn't intend that reflection should be our permanent state. Our lives are to be lived today. The calling on our lives is to be pursued, the message and truth we have to share is to be spread. '**Today is Friday. But Sunday's coming**.'* So today as we rest, reflect and remember, may we remind ourselves of just how much goodness there is to come. We might, in some ways, believe there to be nothing good about 'Good' Friday, but this day actually marked what had only just begun.

*S.M. Lockridge, *That's My King* (YouTube) wvly.org/iwed-15apr21

Thank You, Lord, for Your ultimate sacrifice. Thank You for enduring such scorn and shame – doing it for all of humankind, and doing it for me. Amen.

Weekend

He is risen!

....

Mark 16:1–8

"'Don't be alarmed," he said. "You are looking for Jesus the Nazarene, who was crucified. He has risen! He is not here.'" (v6)

'*He has risen!*' What life-altering words these women were met with that first Easter morning, and what significant ramifications they have for all of us today. Death is defeated, our sins are forgiven, and our perspective on life is forever altered as a result.

Easter Sunday means that as we go about our day-to-day lives, and as we're faced with challenges we might not have seen coming, we have a new stance. Now, we fight *from* victory as opposed to *for* it. Easter Sunday is the ultimate call to cease striving and scraping by on scraps of weary work and from the 'hustle' culture we're acclimatised to.

Today, we're called to feast on His fullness and understand that the battle is won and it is finished. When this isn't what our reality looks like, may we leave our burdens at the cross.

If there was ever a call for radical rest, it's Easter Sunday. There is no greater act than this conquering of sin and death, and there never will be. He did this for me and for you, that we might walk away from the terror the world wants to scare us with into the triumph He won for us.

He is risen indeed!

....

Optional further reading

Matthew 28:1–20; Luke 24:1–12

What **next?**

Matthew 28:16–20

'Therefore go and make disciples of all nations, baptising them in the name of the Father and of the Son and of the Holy Spirit' (v19)

We could absolutely forgive the disciples for their worry, doubt and disbelief, couldn't we? What they'd just been through was littered with both trauma and triumph. They'd watched their friend and Saviour die, only to see Him live again. Yes, He'd said that this would happen, but understanding something theoretically and practically are two very different things, aren't they?

So, what next? The call for the disciples is the same one which exists for you and me today: 'go and make disciples of all nations' (v19a)

Jesus literally walked with the disciples. Day in and day out for three years. It's safe to say that they knew a bit about what He expected from them once He was gone.

We know, too. From this passage, yes, and also from the multitudes of passages and promises which find their 'yes and amen' in Him even today. From our real, rich and raw lived experiences, from the words we've had prayed and prophesied over us, from the people we've met and been poured into by. We know.

We know we're called to work, to rest, to be purposeful, passionate, kind and true. We're called to love because He first loved us, and we're called to hope because of who He is and what He's done.

I can quickly question why the disciples were so bewildered by 'what next?' (Some of them went back to fishing.) But the truth is, unless I make it a habit to call to mind God's truths on a regular basis with some times of real reflection, I too can find myself going back to what I *think* I know best, when the biggest truth and reality is that we all just really need Him.

For Prayer and reflection

Father God, thank You for Your patience with me. Thank You for the fact that, even when You seem distant, You're always with me – leading and guiding my every step. Amen.

Food and rest is **spiritual**

1 Kings 19:1–9

'Get up and eat, for the journey is too much for you.' (v7)

I f there was ever an example of the heart of humanness which we can look to in the face of challenges, especially as leaders, it's the example of Elijah. Picture the scene. He's just killed *hundreds* of Baal prophets and now Jezebel's out to kill *him*. I mean, he's not exactly shown himself to be the shy and retiring type in the whole killing-prophets saga. He's most certainly a leader. And yet now, in light of one woman out for his life, his faith seems to have dwindled.

I think Elijah gives us a clear example of burnout. And despite being in communication with God so consistently and clearly, it's not obviously *spiritual* tools which God provides Elijah to recover with.

I remember when I first properly discovered the 'personal development' world. Having only recently come back to God, I felt nervous about the idea of any kind of development which wasn't backed up with a Bible verse. Don't get me wrong, we have to be hugely discerning when it comes to navigating how we go and grow in the direction of our goals when there's so much information at our fingertips, but there are so many 'natural' and manufactured resources which God has put in our path to help us, even if they're not explicitly attached to Scripture. Rest and food are two of those things.

After a nap and some dinner, Elijah took a 40-day journey (v8), so it's safe to say he felt better, despite previously asking the Lord to take his life (v4). Yes, pray, read the Bible, worship – but don't neglect the very human resources available to you in your pursuit of holiness. They might be exactly where God is leading you.

For Prayer and reflection

What tools and resources do you typically use when you feel weary? Have you found yourself dismissing things like food and rest for fear they're not spiritual enough?

Stay **your** course

Productivity is one of those buzz words everyone talks about, isn't it? 'Wake up at 5am.' 'Have a cold shower.' 'Turn your phone notifications off.' 'Listen to this podcast.' 'Read that book.'

Whilst I understand how all, or at least some of these methods might be helpful in the pursuit and practice of productivity, I believe that one of the most powerful ways of propelling us into productivity is to pursue *true* purpose. Right from verse 1 of the book of Nehemiah, we see that he felt a real burden for this work of rebuilding the wall (see 1:3–4). So it's no surprise to hear that what kickstarted him and kept him going was the sense of purpose and passion he had for the cause he was committed to.

There have been times in my life when I've asked myself what more I can do or implement in order to *achieve* more. There have also been times when I've had to remind myself to take breaks, recharge and stop because the work I've been doing has felt so much like non-work that I've almost forgotten it was work.

Whilst both of these examples have their own challenges, sometimes – rather than trying to muster up the strength and stamina to keep doing work, which might no longer be what the Lord is leading you in the direction of – ask Him instead what His will is for your work and how He wants you to use your time. You might then find yourself less distracted and dissuaded, just like Nehemiah was, when the enemy wants to knock you off course and get you doing something else. When you *know* that the work you're doing is the work you're meant to be doing, productivity will have much more purpose.

....
Nehemiah 6:1–9
....

'I am carrying on a great project and cannot go down. Why should the work stop while I leave it and go down to you?' (v3)

....
For Prayer and reflection
....

Lord, I pray that You'll reveal to me Your desire for my life, and help me to easily discern distraction and enable me to stay in my lane as I serve You. Amen.

Purpose is **powerful**

John 7:25–31

'At this they tried to seize him, but no one laid a hand on him, because his hour had not yet come.' (v30)

Following on from yesterday, today's passage gives us a great example of how purpose can actually protect us. I don't mean the purpose itself, but more the sense that when God is for us – for something we're doing, a message we're sharing etc – who can be against us (see Rom. 8:31)?

At the point we've reached in today's passage, there's real division regarding who Jesus is. Many people want to kill Him, or at least keep Him quiet, and this all comes to a head when we see people trying to arrest Him. None of it was effective because 'his hour had not yet come' (v30). When God is calling you to do something, it may seem risky, counter-cultural, daunting and even impossible. The good news is that those risks and challenges won't be able to come to anything substantial without God's say so when you're walking in purpose.

The flip side of that is also positive. When challenges and trials come our way, even when we know that we *are* walking in purpose, we get to lean in and listen to them a little. Don't get me wrong, no trial is nice. But when purpose is in pole position and we're presented with a challenge anyway, we can ask God what He might want to teach us, or where He might want to be leading us. Knowing that what we're doing is for the Lord eliminates our need to question or contemplate if we've made a mistake or if we've not heard God correctly. Instead, we get to show up boldly and brightly without shrinking back, trusting and knowing that whatever comes our way is something which is going to help us better listen and learn, and that it will ultimately be for His glory and our good.

For Prayer and reflection

Father, I thank You that as I walk in step with Your Holy Spirit, and in line with Your will for my life, I am protected by You at all times. Thank You, Lord. Amen.

Celebrating success

Psalm 126

'The LORD has done great things for us, and we are filled with joy.' (v3)

f you're anything like me, you may well find yourself reaching one goal and then immediately wondering what it's going to take for you to reach your next one.

We're not a people who are great with being able to take stock and pause. Often, our 'hustle harder' culture can have us thinking that we're human doings as opposed to human beings. It's almost as though we're wired to believe (often subconsciously) that we're cogs on the machine and that without producing more, at all times, we don't have a sense of value.

An excellent way to resist believing this lie is to ensure that we pause in order to celebrate, whenever we achieve a small 'win'.

Many of us will have long-term goals and pursuits which aren't going to be achieved overnight. However, as we continue to take steps in the direction of our declarations, we'll no doubt overcome and achieve certain things along the way.

Thank the Lord for these victories – however small.

Pause, take stock, pray and worship – just like in the example we see here from the psalmist.

There isn't a prerequisite on what actually constitutes a 'win', and the chances are you're being hard on yourself by overlooking seemingly small victories in favour of looking towards the next thing you want to tick off your to-do list.

Resist the urge. Instead, thank the Lord for the great things He has done and has enabled you to do. Allow your 'cup' to be filled with joy, just as the psalmist's was.

There's always going to be more to do, but there's not always going to be this moment to just be – so take it with open arms.

For Prayer and reflection

How will you be pausing and taking stock today, in order to celebrate what you've already achieved *before* you move on to ticking the next thing off your to-do list?

Courageous and unsure – a poem

....

Deuteronomy 31:1–6

'Be strong and courageous... for the LORD your God goes with you' (v6)

realised I'd forgotten the last time I cried.
At first, I felt satisfied.
Proud of the work I'd done to heal...
Until I recognised it's not *wrong* to feel.
When things are painful, it's okay to show it.
If you're still working it out, it's okay not to know it.
Band aid on brokenness = more mess.
So, what am I saying?
That it's fine to feel anger even whilst you're praying.
That it's both/and, not either/or.
That you can truly be courageous alongside unsure.
Now of course, with the feelings, you still get to choose.
A life of emotion isn't a sentence of blues.
You get to decide.
Hide your pride and go all in for you.
Take what's *true* and own it.

The tears, the joy, you *grow* through it.
And what have you learned?
What can you take from your heart being churned?
What's your post-rejection journey of introspection?
What type of reflection serves your new direction?
Where do you land?
After taking this path, knowing it's been planned.
You're never left or forsaken, even when you're mistaken.
Lean in and feel that.
Let those layers peel back.
Then go again, having KNOWN the walk you've been shown.
Don't stop going. Don't stop growing.
Let your authentic LIFE be what is showing.

· ·

Optional further reading
Matthew 6:25–35; Romans 7:15–20

Burnout and **boundaries**

1 Peter 5:6–9

'Be alert and of sober mind. Your enemy the devil prowls around like a roaring lion looking for someone to devour.' (v8)

I'm not typically one to quote Star Trek, but I will say that when it comes to the will and the ways of the enemy, resistance is most certainly *not* futile. Although this might sound as though it's quite a gloomy message, it's an important one – especially with all we've been discussing in relation to pursuing purpose.

The devil is called our enemy for a reason. He doesn't want us to win or succeed at anything, because when we live out the work we're called to do in the way the Lord would have us do it, we are glorifying God, which the enemy hates.

Although nothing can happen without God's say so (see the book of Job), we're not called to shut our eyes and pretend that the enemy doesn't exist as we go about our day-to-day routine.

I believe that if there was ever a verse which called for radical rest, it's this one. Although that might seem strange at first, picture the scene. You're up to your eyeballs with work and the deadlines are looming and lingering, you haven't eaten all day because of said deadlines, and you know it's time to go and pick your kids up from school. Kids who, by the way, you haven't sorted any dinner for yet. Tired is an understatement. You needed a break yesterday, but there's not one sight.

Who more susceptible than a burnt out and boundaryless person for the enemy to pounce on as he prowls? Whispers of ease and surface-level satisfaction certainly scream louder when we're at the end of ourselves, which means that being 'alert' and 'of sober mind' is more important than ever – even and perhaps especially when we're weary. Making room for rest is active resistance.

For Prayer and reflection

What boundaries do you have in place to ensure that you don't burn out amidst the busyness of your daily life? How do you ensure you stick to them?

Next Issue

MAY/JUN 2022

May

MERCY BRINGERS

NATALIE WILLIAMS

June

YOUR NAME IS BETTER

EMMA SCRIVENER

Inspiring **Women** Every Day

MERCY BRINGERS
NATALIE WILLIAMS

YOUR NAME IS BETTER
EMMA SCRIVENER

Daily devotional by women for women

Available in a variety of formats

In **May**, join Natalie Williams to explore God's mercy and His desire for you to be a mercy-bringer. Getting to grips with this undeserved loving kindness can transform your heart, attitude and actions in unexpected ways.

In **June**, Emma Scrivener asks an important question: "Who do you think you are?" Explore the power of a name, who you are and where you belong. What does God call you and how does your identity given by Christ impact your life?

Get your copy from waverleyabbeyresources.org

Abide

John 15:1–17

'Neither can you
bear fruit unless
you remain in me.'
(v4)

'm the first to talk about how useful self-help/
personal development books, videos and courses
can be. However, I'm aware that, without the Lord,
our attempts to help ourselves won't amount to much.

Today's passage makes it abundantly clear that we
need the Lord and that, without Him, our 'fruit' is going
to look a lot more forced than flourishing.

What I find really comforting about today's passage
is that it says, 'Remain in me, *as I also remain in you*'
(v4a, italics added). What a powerful reminder that God
is immovable and unchangeable, even in the midst of
some of our most difficult situations. It is always us who
moves and shifts. I wonder if you, like me, can relate to
this?

I've always valued competence and strength in
leadership and hope that I'm able to portray some of
these qualities in anything I'm leading. However, there
have certainly been times in my life when, because of an
opportunity God has given me to use my gifts, I've later
thought that this means it's just something natural within
me. I've been rudely awoken when I've gone to replicate
something similar in my own strength and haven't had
the same results.

Yes, of course we'll be able to muster up the energy
to do something we're familiar with, or are trained in, if
we really need to. But we don't need to push ourselves
in that way. 'Doing' often comes so much more easily
when we're operating from a place of abiding in Him
as He abides in us. Allow that to be a relief today, as
opposed to a suggestion that you're 'weak'. The truth
is, we all are -— but the good news is that He is anything
but.

**For Prayer
and reflection**

**Thank You, Lord,
for the gift You
have given me of
being able to work,
create and build. I
pray that I won't
do any of this
apart from You.
Keep me close, I
pray. Amen.**

The surrender in **slumber**

I f there was ever an example to take heed of when it comes to the subject of radical rest, it's that of Jesus in the boat with His disciples in the midst of a torrential storm. Whilst we're often pointed to the response of the disciples to the storm and their apparent lack of faith, what I love is the attitude of Jesus in the midst of this raging tempest.

Being all-knowing, Jesus must have foreseen that a storm was on its way. But rather than changing the plans and getting everyone to turn back, He simply gets in the boat. Not only does He get in the boat, but He swiftly proceeds to fall asleep as He does so.

Verse 23 makes it clear that the disciples had good reason to be nervous, for 'they were in great danger'. Strangely, this is actually one of the most comforting aspects of the passage to me.

When *we're* in great danger (perceived or actual), Jesus is in the metaphorical boat with us. Not only that, He's resting. He's not going to allow anything to happen without His say so and therefore He's not at all threatened by the wind and the waves, no matter how hard they hit. What's more, though, is that the wind and the waves are threatened by Him.

Jesus quickly calms the storm and questions the disciples' faith. I don't see this so much as a rebuke, as I do a genuine question – a challenge, if you will.

Where is my faith when things get rocky? Has Jesus suddenly left me? Of course not! He's promised His eternal presence with us, no matter what. So, when we're unable to rest in the eye of the storm, may we look to Him who does.

Luke 8:22–25

'As they sailed, he fell asleep. A squall came down on the lake, so that the boat was being swamped' (v23)

For Prayer and reflection

Is there a storm I'm currently facing, where I've forgotten who's in the boat with me as I go through it? How can I exercise faith today knowing that Jesus is with me?

The **ease** and the effort

Ephesians 4:1–7

'As a prisoner for the Lord, then, I urge you to live a life worthy of the calling you have received.' (v1)

I've always been moved and compelled by the words Paul speaks in this passage. At times of tiredness and terror, I've felt somewhat mocked by them. What does it mean to 'make every effort' when we're broken and beaten down by life? Other times, when I'm motivated and mobilised, I've felt inspired by these words – 'of *course* I'm able to make efforts towards the life God's called me to live because look how "well" I'm doing right now, and how much I've been able to produce recently'.

The truth of the matter is that none of these responses is actually what I think Paul was trying to get at here. My old pastor always used to say of the Bible, 'When we see a 'therefore', we have to know what it's there for'. That's really stuck with me.

Before this moment, we read of Paul praying for *spiritual* strength. It's such a rich and passionate prayer (see 3:14–21). He's in a literal prison at the time. He's praying for himself, yes, but also for all of the saints. Back to our passage, he urges us to walk in unity, peace, humility, patience and gentleness.

My initial thought process around this passage falls short because I interpret the word 'effort' to mean my striving, pushing and hustle. Actually, the effort isn't about reaching a position or a platform at all. The effort is to allow His everlasting arms to be what strengthen ours when we don't feel we have what it takes any more. We're not supposed to. Whatever context we're called to – company CEO, stay-at-home parent, itinerant worker – the call is the same. Love God and love His people – with *His* love and *His* strength.

For Prayer and reflection

Thank You, Lord, that the main effort which You call us to is one of remembering that it's You who's carrying us. Please cease our striving and turn us to trust. Amen.

Such love, is this for **me?**

'll always have a special relationship with Psalm 139. In my days as a secondary school teacher, there was a season where I led an alternative education provision and actually taught in a church. This meant that at break and lunch times, Bibles were lying around and, occasionally, a student would pick one up and have a flick through.

On seeing one of the students pick up a Bible one day, a colleague of mine called to her to take a look at Psalm 139. She read it and smiled. I didn't think much more of it.

A week or so later, I was presented with a tea-stained piece of paper from the same student. She said to me, 'I really loved this and wanted to write it out. I felt something when I read it and I wanted to give this to you.' Needless to say, I put this same precious piece of paper in a frame.

How powerful to think that God's Word could reach out and communicate to a student without a faith to speak of, and cause her to think about it further and feel something as she did so.

It can be so tempting to view the Bible as simply another book on the shelf, and yet it's the living and active Word of God. Hebrews 4:12 tells us that it discerns the thoughts and intentions of our heart. It reads us as we read it.

When we allow for our daily routine to include even a moment of reflection and rest in the Word, we can often get a lot more than we bargained for as the Lord meets us exactly where we're at and, often, seemingly with exactly what we need. As we read His Word today, may we be reminded of its power, and the Lord's presence in its pages.

Psalm 139:1–10

'You hem me in behind and before, and you lay your hand upon me.'
(v5)

For Prayer and reflection

Thank You, Lord, for Your Word, for both the power and the peace we find in it. May we never neglect to read Your Word and, in doing so, allow it to read us. Amen.

Weekend

Life to the full

....

John 10:7–10

'I have come that they may have life, and have it to the full.' (v10)

When we think about routine and direction which is oriented in purpose, *as well as* maintaining boundaries so as to ensure rest and rejuvenation, we can begin to have thoughts which sound like 'that's too idealistic' and 'who do you think you are for wondering if your life could look like that?' As we round up this month, I'd like to suggest that these thoughts are lies, and not ones which we need to entertain.

John 10:10 has long been one of my favourite verses. It reminds me of the truth when I start to wonder if I'm making the right choices or thinking too big. We know that, as believers, we won't be free from trouble in this world (see John 16:33), but this verse is a welcome reminder that we don't have to live feeling afraid or uncertain.

Yes, the enemy wants to rob us of our peace and our purpose every single day, but we don't have to dwell on that. We get to fix our eyes on the fact that Jesus doesn't intend us to live life hanging on by a thread. He longs for us to live life to the *full* – His glorious fullness. Let's walk in this truth today and always.

....

Optional further reading

Psalm 16

Order form

Get Your **FREE** Daily Bible Reading Notes **TODAY!** (UK ONLY)

Your favourite Bible reading notes are now FREE. God has called us back to the original vision of CWR to provide these notes to everyone who needs them, regardless of their circumstance or ability to pay. It is our desire to see these daily Bible reading notes used more widely, to see Christians grow in their relationship with Jesus on a daily basis and to see Him reflected in their everyday living. Clearly there are costs to provide this ministry and we are trusting in God's provision.

Could you be part of this vision? Do you have the desire to see lives transformed through a relationship with Jesus? **A small donation from you of just £2 a month, by direct debit, will make such a difference** Giving hope to someone in desperate need whilst you too grow deeper in your own relationship with Jesus.

4 Easy Ways To Order

1. Visit our online store at **waverleyabbeyresources.org/store**
2. Send this form together with your payment to: **Waverley Abbey Trust, Waverley Abbey House, Waverley Lane, Farnham, Surrey GU9 8EP**
3. Phone in your credit card order: **01252 784700** (Mon–Fri, 9.30am – 4.30pm)
4. Visit a Christian bookshop

For a list of our National Distributors, who supply countries outside the UK, visit waverleyabbeyresources.org/distributors

Your Details (required for orders and donations)

Full Name:	ID No. (if known):
Home Address:	
	Postcode:
Telephone No. (for queries):	Email:

Publications

TITLE	QTY	PRICE	TOTAL
		TOTAL PUBLICATIONS	

UK P&P: up to £24.99 = **£2.99**; £25.00 and over = **FREE**	
Elsewhere P&P: up to £10 = **£4.95**; £10.01 – £50 = **£6.95**; £50.01 – £99.99 = **£10**; £100 and over = **£30**	
Total Publications and P&P (please allow 14 days for delivery)	**A**

Payment Details

☐ I enclose a cheque made payable to CWR for the amount of: **£** _____

☐ Please charge my credit/debit card.

Cardholder's Name (in BLOCK CAPITALS) _____

Card No. ☐☐☐☐ ☐☐☐☐ ☐☐☐☐ ☐☐☐☐

Expires End ☐☐ ☐☐   Security Code ☐☐☐

Continued overleaf >>

<< See previous page for start of order form

One off Special Gift to Waverley Abbey Trust   ☐ Please send me an acknowledgement of my gift   **B** [   ]

GRAND TOTAL (Total of A & B) [   ]

Gift Aid (your home address required, see overleaf)

giftaid it   I am a UK taxpayer and want CWR to reclaim the tax on all my donations for the four years prior to this year **and on** all donations I make from the date of this Gift Aid declaration until further notice.*

Taxpayer's Full Name (in BLOCK CAPITALS) _____

Signature _____   **Date** _____

*I am a UK taxpayer and understand that if I pay less Income Tax and/or Capital Gains Tax than the amount of Gift Aid claimed on all my donations in that tax year it is my responsibility to pay any difference.

Your FREE Daily Bible Reading Notes Order

	Please Tick	FREE	£2 pcm	£5 pcm	£10 pcm	Other
Every Day with Jesus		☐	☐	☐	☐	☐ £ ___
Large Print *Every Day with Jesus*		☐	☐	☐	☐	☐ £ ___
Inspiring Women Every Day		☐	☐	☐	☐	☐ £ ___

All CWR Bible reading notes are also available in single issue **ebook** and **email subscription** format. Visit **waverleyabbeyresources.org** for further info.

CWR Instruction to your Bank or Building Society to pay by Direct Debit

DIRECT Debit

Please fill in the form and send to: CWR, Waverley Abbey House, Waverley Lane, Farnham, Surrey GU9 8EP

Name and full postal address of your Bank or Building Society

To: The Manager   Bank/Building Society

Address _____

_____

Postcode _____

Originator's Identification Number

4	2	0	4	8	7

Reference

[| | | | | | | | | | | | | | |]

Instruction to your Bank or Building Society

Please pay CWR Direct Debits from the account detailed in this Instructi[on] subject to the safeguards assured by the Direct Debit Guarantee. I understand that this Instruction may remain with CWR and, if so, details will be passed electronically to my Bank/Building Society.

Name(s) of Account Holder(s)

[   ]

Branch Sort Code

[| | | | |]

Signature(s)

[   ]

Bank/Building Society Account Number

[| | | | | | |]

Date

Banks and Building Societies may not accept Direct Debit Instructions for some types of account

For a subscription outside of the UK please visit www.waverleyabbeyresources.org where you will find a list of our national distributors.

How would you like to hear from us? We would love to keep you up to date on all aspects of the CWR ministry, including; new publications, events & courses as well as how you can support us.

If you **DO** want to hear from us on email, please tick here [ ] If you **DO NOT** want us to contact you by post, please tick here [ ]

You can update your preferences at any time by contacting our customer services team on 01252 784 700. You can view our privacy policy online at waverleyabbeyresources.org